# 50 Hearty Winter Soups Recipes for Home

By: Kelly Johnson

# Table of Contents

- Classic Chicken Noodle Soup
- Beef and Barley Soup
- Creamy Tomato Basil Soup
- Butternut Squash Soup
- Lentil and Sausage Soup
- Minestrone Soup
- French Onion Soup
- Potato Leek Soup
- Split Pea Soup with Ham
- White Bean and Kale Soup
- Roasted Red Pepper and Tomato Soup
- Chicken and Wild Rice Soup
- Italian Wedding Soup
- Corn Chowder
- Spicy Pumpkin Soup
- Mushroom and Barley Soup
- Turkey and Vegetable Soup
- Ham and Potato Chowder
- Broccoli Cheddar Soup
- Cabbage Roll Soup
- Moroccan Chickpea Soup
- Chili con Carne
- Chicken Tortilla Soup
- Sweet Potato and Black Bean Soup
- Lemon Chicken Orzo Soup
- Creamy Cauliflower Soup
- Sausage and Kale Soup
- Coconut Curry Chicken Soup
- Quinoa Vegetable Soup
- Three-Bean Chili
- Cream of Asparagus Soup
- Italian Sausage and Tortellini Soup
- Ginger Carrot Soup
- Beef Stew with Root Vegetables
- Spinach and White Bean Soup

- Thai Tom Yum Soup
- Chicken and Dumplings
- Roasted Garlic and Potato Soup
- Wild Mushroom Bisque
- Seafood Chowder
- Lemon Lentil Soup
- Mexican Street Corn Soup
- Tuscan White Bean Soup
- Roasted Pumpkin and Sage Soup
- Chicken Gumbo
- Tomato and Basil Bisque
- Black Bean and Chorizo Soup
- Lemon Artichoke Soup
- Hungarian Goulash Soup
- Spaghetti Squash and Meatball Soup

**Classic Chicken Noodle Soup**

Ingredients:

- 1 tablespoon olive oil
- 1 onion, finely chopped
- 2 carrots, sliced
- 2 celery stalks, sliced
- 3 cloves garlic, minced
- 1 teaspoon dried thyme
- 1 teaspoon dried rosemary
- 6 cups chicken broth
- 2 cups cooked shredded chicken (rotisserie chicken works well)
- 2 cups egg noodles
- Salt and pepper to taste
- Fresh parsley, chopped (for garnish)

Instructions:

In a large pot, heat the olive oil over medium heat. Add the chopped onion, carrots, and celery. Sauté until the vegetables are softened, about 5-7 minutes. Add the minced garlic, dried thyme, and dried rosemary. Cook for an additional 1-2 minutes until the garlic is fragrant.

Pour in the chicken broth and bring the mixture to a boil. Reduce the heat to simmer.

Add the shredded chicken to the pot and let it simmer for about 10 minutes to allow the flavors to meld.

Meanwhile, cook the egg noodles according to the package instructions in a separate pot. Drain and set aside.

Add the cooked noodles to the soup. Season with salt and pepper to taste. Let the soup simmer for an additional 5-10 minutes until heated through.

Taste and adjust the seasoning as needed. If the soup is too thick, you can add more chicken broth.

Ladle the soup into bowls, garnish with fresh parsley, and serve hot.

This classic chicken noodle soup is not only delicious but also a great remedy for colds or just a comforting meal any day. Feel free to customize it by adding extra vegetables or herbs to suit your taste.

**Beef and Barley Soup**

Ingredients:

- 1 tablespoon olive oil
- 1.5 lbs (680g) beef stew meat, cut into bite-sized pieces
- Salt and pepper to taste
- 1 onion, finely chopped
- 2 carrots, sliced
- 2 celery stalks, sliced
- 3 cloves garlic, minced
- 1 teaspoon dried thyme
- 1 teaspoon dried rosemary
- 1 cup pearl barley, rinsed
- 8 cups beef broth
- 2 bay leaves
- 2 cups chopped tomatoes (canned or fresh)
- 1 cup frozen peas
- Fresh parsley, chopped (for garnish)

Instructions:

In a large pot, heat the olive oil over medium-high heat. Season the beef stew meat with salt and pepper, then brown the meat in batches. Remove the browned meat and set it aside.

In the same pot, add a bit more oil if needed and sauté the chopped onion, carrots, and celery until softened.

Add the minced garlic, dried thyme, and dried rosemary. Cook for an additional 1-2 minutes until the garlic is fragrant.

Return the browned beef to the pot. Add the rinsed barley, beef broth, bay leaves, and chopped tomatoes. Bring the mixture to a boil.

Reduce the heat to low, cover the pot, and let it simmer for about 1 to 1.5 hours or until the beef is tender and the barley is cooked through.

About 15 minutes before serving, add the frozen peas to the soup and continue simmering until they are heated through.

Taste the soup and adjust the seasoning as needed. Remove the bay leaves before serving.

Ladle the beef and barley soup into bowls, garnish with fresh parsley, and serve hot.

This hearty soup is not only delicious but also nutritious with the combination of beef, barley, and vegetables. It's a comforting meal that will warm you up on a cold winter day. Enjoy!

**Creamy Tomato Basil Soup**

Ingredients:

- 2 tablespoons olive oil
- 1 onion, chopped
- 2 carrots, peeled and chopped
- 2 celery stalks, chopped
- 3 cloves garlic, minced
- 2 cans (28 ounces each) whole peeled tomatoes
- 1 can (14 ounces) crushed tomatoes
- 1 teaspoon dried basil
- 1 teaspoon dried oregano
- 1/2 teaspoon dried thyme
- 4 cups vegetable or chicken broth
- Salt and pepper to taste
- 1/2 cup heavy cream
- Fresh basil leaves, for garnish
- Grated Parmesan cheese, for garnish

Instructions:

In a large pot, heat the olive oil over medium heat. Add the chopped onion, carrots, and celery. Sauté until the vegetables are softened, about 5-7 minutes.
Add the minced garlic and cook for an additional 1-2 minutes until fragrant.
Pour in the whole peeled tomatoes and crushed tomatoes. Break apart the whole tomatoes using a spoon or spatula.
Add the dried basil, oregano, and thyme to the pot. Stir to combine.
Pour in the vegetable or chicken broth and bring the mixture to a simmer. Let it simmer for about 20-25 minutes to allow the flavors to meld.
Use an immersion blender to blend the soup until smooth. Alternatively, transfer the soup in batches to a blender, blend, and return it to the pot.
Season the soup with salt and pepper to taste.
Stir in the heavy cream, and let the soup simmer for an additional 5 minutes.
Taste and adjust the seasoning if necessary.
Ladle the creamy tomato basil soup into bowls, garnish with fresh basil leaves and grated Parmesan cheese.

Serve this creamy and flavorful soup with a slice of crusty bread for a delightful winter meal. Enjoy!

**Butternut Squash Soup**

Ingredients:

- 1 large butternut squash, peeled, seeded, and diced (about 4 cups)
- 2 tablespoons olive oil
- 1 onion, chopped
- 2 carrots, peeled and chopped
- 2 celery stalks, chopped
- 3 cloves garlic, minced
- 1 teaspoon ground cumin
- 1/2 teaspoon ground cinnamon
- 1/4 teaspoon ground nutmeg
- 4 cups vegetable or chicken broth
- Salt and pepper to taste
- 1 cup coconut milk or heavy cream
- 1 tablespoon maple syrup (optional)
- Toasted pumpkin seeds, for garnish
- Fresh parsley or chives, chopped (for garnish)

Instructions:

Preheat the oven to 400°F (200°C).
Place the diced butternut squash on a baking sheet, drizzle with olive oil, and season with salt and pepper. Toss to coat evenly. Roast in the preheated oven for about 30-35 minutes or until the squash is tender and lightly caramelized.
In a large pot, heat olive oil over medium heat. Add the chopped onion, carrots, and celery. Sauté until the vegetables are softened, about 5-7 minutes.
Add the minced garlic, ground cumin, ground cinnamon, and ground nutmeg. Cook for an additional 1-2 minutes until the spices are fragrant.
Add the roasted butternut squash to the pot and pour in the vegetable or chicken broth. Bring the mixture to a simmer and let it cook for about 10-15 minutes to allow the flavors to meld.
Use an immersion blender to blend the soup until smooth. Alternatively, transfer the soup in batches to a blender, blend, and return it to the pot.
Stir in the coconut milk or heavy cream. If desired, add maple syrup for a touch of sweetness. Season with additional salt and pepper to taste.
Let the soup simmer for an additional 5 minutes.

Ladle the butternut squash soup into bowls, garnish with toasted pumpkin seeds and chopped fresh parsley or chives.

This creamy and flavorful butternut squash soup is perfect for a cozy winter evening.

Enjoy with a slice of crusty bread or as an appetizer for a larger meal.

**Lentil and Sausage Soup**

Ingredients:

- 1 cup dried green or brown lentils, rinsed and drained
- 1 tablespoon olive oil
- 1 onion, chopped
- 2 carrots, peeled and chopped
- 2 celery stalks, chopped
- 3 cloves garlic, minced
- 1 pound (450g) Italian sausage, casings removed
- 1 teaspoon dried oregano
- 1 teaspoon dried thyme
- 1 teaspoon smoked paprika
- 1 can (14 ounces) diced tomatoes
- 6 cups chicken or vegetable broth
- Salt and pepper to taste
- 2 cups chopped kale or spinach
- 1 tablespoon red wine vinegar
- Grated Parmesan cheese, for serving

Instructions:

In a large pot, heat olive oil over medium heat. Add the chopped onion, carrots, and celery. Sauté until the vegetables are softened, about 5-7 minutes.
Add the minced garlic and cook for an additional 1-2 minutes until fragrant.
Add the Italian sausage to the pot, breaking it apart with a spoon as it cooks.
Cook until the sausage is browned and cooked through.
Stir in the dried oregano, dried thyme, and smoked paprika, allowing the spices to coat the sausage and vegetables.
Add the rinsed lentils, diced tomatoes, and chicken or vegetable broth to the pot.
Bring the mixture to a boil, then reduce the heat to simmer.
Cover the pot and let the soup simmer for about 25-30 minutes or until the lentils are tender.
Season the soup with salt and pepper to taste.
Stir in the chopped kale or spinach and let it wilt into the soup.
Just before serving, stir in the red wine vinegar to brighten the flavors.

Ladle the lentil and sausage soup into bowls and serve with a sprinkle of grated Parmesan cheese on top.

This flavorful and protein-packed soup is perfect for a satisfying winter meal. Enjoy with some crusty bread on the side for a complete and hearty experience!

**Minestrone Soup**

Ingredients:

- 2 tablespoons olive oil
- 1 onion, diced
- 2 carrots, peeled and diced
- 2 celery stalks, diced
- 3 cloves garlic, minced
- 1 zucchini, diced
- 1 cup green beans, chopped
- 1 can (14 ounces) diced tomatoes
- 1 can (15 ounces) kidney beans, drained and rinsed
- 1 can (15 ounces) cannellini beans, drained and rinsed
- 1/2 cup small pasta (such as ditalini or elbow)
- 1 teaspoon dried oregano
- 1 teaspoon dried basil
- 1/2 teaspoon dried thyme
- 4 cups vegetable broth
- 2 cups water
- Salt and pepper to taste
- 2 cups chopped spinach or kale
- Grated Parmesan cheese, for serving

Instructions:

In a large pot, heat olive oil over medium heat. Add the diced onion, carrots, and celery. Sauté until the vegetables are softened, about 5-7 minutes.
Add the minced garlic and cook for an additional 1-2 minutes until fragrant.
Stir in the diced zucchini, green beans, diced tomatoes, kidney beans, cannellini beans, and pasta.
Add the dried oregano, dried basil, and dried thyme. Mix well to combine.
Pour in the vegetable broth and water. Bring the soup to a boil, then reduce the heat to simmer.
Season the soup with salt and pepper to taste.
Cover the pot and let the soup simmer for about 15-20 minutes or until the pasta and vegetables are tender.
Stir in the chopped spinach or kale and cook until wilted.

Taste and adjust the seasoning if needed.
Ladle the minestrone soup into bowls and serve with a sprinkle of grated Parmesan cheese on top.

This Minestrone Soup is a comforting and wholesome meal. Enjoy it with a side of crusty bread for a complete and satisfying experience!

**French Onion Soup**

Ingredients:

- 4 large onions, thinly sliced
- 3 tablespoons butter
- 2 tablespoons olive oil
- 1 teaspoon sugar
- 2 cloves garlic, minced
- 1/2 cup dry white wine (optional)
- 4 cups beef broth
- 2 cups chicken broth
- 1 bay leaf
- 1 teaspoon dried thyme
- Salt and pepper to taste
- Baguette slices, toasted
- 2 cups Gruyere or Swiss cheese, shredded

Instructions:

In a large pot, melt butter and olive oil over medium heat. Add the thinly sliced onions and cook, stirring occasionally, until the onions are soft and golden brown. This process may take about 30-40 minutes.

Sprinkle sugar over the caramelized onions to enhance the browning process. Be careful not to burn the sugar.

Add minced garlic to the pot and cook for an additional 1-2 minutes until fragrant.

Pour in the white wine (if using) to deglaze the pot, scraping up any browned bits from the bottom.

Add both beef and chicken broths, bay leaf, dried thyme, salt, and pepper. Bring the soup to a simmer, then reduce the heat to low and let it simmer for about 20-30 minutes to allow the flavors to meld.

Preheat your broiler.

Remove the bay leaf from the soup and taste to adjust the seasoning if necessary.

Ladle the hot soup into oven-safe bowls. Place toasted baguette slices on top of the soup.

Sprinkle a generous amount of shredded Gruyere or Swiss cheese over each bowl.

Place the bowls on a baking sheet and broil until the cheese is melted and bubbly, with a golden-brown crust.
Carefully remove the bowls from the oven, allowing them to cool slightly before serving.

Serve this classic French Onion Soup hot, and enjoy the gooey cheese and rich broth with each spoonful. It's perfect for a cozy winter evening.

**Potato Leek Soup**

Ingredients:

- 3 leeks, white and light green parts only, sliced
- 3 tablespoons butter
- 3 large potatoes, peeled and diced
- 4 cups vegetable or chicken broth
- 1 bay leaf
- 1 teaspoon dried thyme
- Salt and pepper to taste
- 1 cup whole milk or heavy cream
- Chives or parsley, chopped (for garnish)

Instructions:

In a large pot, melt the butter over medium heat. Add the sliced leeks and cook until softened, about 5-7 minutes.

Add the diced potatoes to the pot and cook for an additional 5 minutes, stirring occasionally.

Pour in the vegetable or chicken broth, add the bay leaf and dried thyme. Season with salt and pepper to taste.

Bring the soup to a boil, then reduce the heat to low and let it simmer for about 15-20 minutes or until the potatoes are tender.

Remove the bay leaf from the pot.

Use an immersion blender to blend the soup until smooth. Alternatively, transfer the soup in batches to a blender, blend, and return it to the pot.

Stir in the whole milk or heavy cream, and let the soup simmer for an additional 5 minutes.

Taste and adjust the seasoning if necessary.

Ladle the potato leek soup into bowls, garnish with chopped chives or parsley, and serve hot.

This creamy and satisfying Potato Leek Soup is perfect for a simple and comforting winter meal. Pair it with a slice of crusty bread for a delightful experience. Enjoy!

**Split Pea Soup with Ham**

Ingredients:

- 1 pound (about 2 cups) dried split peas, rinsed and drained
- 2 tablespoons olive oil
- 1 onion, chopped
- 2 carrots, peeled and diced
- 2 celery stalks, diced
- 3 cloves garlic, minced
- 1 ham bone or 1-2 cups diced cooked ham
- 8 cups chicken or vegetable broth
- 2 bay leaves
- 1 teaspoon dried thyme
- Salt and pepper to taste
- 1 cup potatoes, peeled and diced
- 1 cup frozen green peas
- Fresh parsley, chopped (for garnish)

Instructions:

In a large pot, heat olive oil over medium heat. Add the chopped onion, carrots, and celery. Sauté until the vegetables are softened, about 5-7 minutes.
Add the minced garlic and cook for an additional 1-2 minutes until fragrant.
Add the rinsed split peas, ham bone or diced ham, chicken or vegetable broth, bay leaves, and dried thyme to the pot. Stir to combine.
Bring the soup to a boil, then reduce the heat to low, cover, and let it simmer for about 1 to 1.5 hours, or until the split peas are tender and the soup has thickened.
Remove the ham bone from the soup. If using diced ham, leave it in the soup.
Season the soup with salt and pepper to taste.
Add the diced potatoes and frozen green peas to the pot. Continue simmering for an additional 15-20 minutes or until the potatoes are tender.
Taste and adjust the seasoning if necessary.
Ladle the split pea soup into bowls, garnish with chopped fresh parsley, and serve hot.

This Split Pea Soup with Ham is a comforting and nutritious dish that's sure to warm you up on a cold winter day. Enjoy it with a slice of crusty bread for a complete meal.

**White Bean and Kale Soup**

Ingredients:

- 2 tablespoons olive oil
- 1 onion, chopped
- 2 carrots, peeled and diced
- 3 cloves garlic, minced
- 2 cans (15 ounces each) white beans (cannellini or Great Northern), drained and rinsed
- 1 bunch kale, stems removed and leaves chopped
- 4 cups vegetable or chicken broth
- 1 teaspoon dried thyme
- 1 teaspoon dried rosemary
- Salt and pepper to taste
- 1 can (14 ounces) diced tomatoes
- 1 Parmesan rind (optional)
- Zest of 1 lemon
- Juice of 1 lemon
- Grated Parmesan cheese, for serving

Instructions:

In a large pot, heat the olive oil over medium heat. Add the chopped onion and carrots. Sauté until the vegetables are softened, about 5-7 minutes.
Add the minced garlic and cook for an additional 1-2 minutes until fragrant.
Stir in the white beans, chopped kale, vegetable or chicken broth, dried thyme, dried rosemary, salt, and pepper.
Add the diced tomatoes (with their juices) and the Parmesan rind (if using). Stir to combine.
Bring the soup to a boil, then reduce the heat to low and let it simmer for about 15-20 minutes, or until the kale is tender.
Remove the Parmesan rind from the pot.
Stir in the lemon zest and lemon juice. Taste and adjust the seasoning if necessary.
Ladle the white bean and kale soup into bowls, and serve hot with a sprinkle of grated Parmesan cheese on top.

This hearty and nutritious soup is not only delicious but also a great way to incorporate healthy greens into your winter diet. Enjoy it with some crusty bread for a satisfying and wholesome meal!

**Roasted Red Pepper and Tomato Soup**

Ingredients:

- 3 red bell peppers, halved and seeds removed
- 2 tablespoons olive oil
- 1 onion, chopped
- 3 cloves garlic, minced
- 2 cans (28 ounces each) whole peeled tomatoes
- 4 cups vegetable or chicken broth
- 1 teaspoon dried basil
- 1 teaspoon dried oregano
- Salt and pepper to taste
- 1/2 cup heavy cream (optional)
- Fresh basil leaves, for garnish
- Croutons, for serving

Instructions:

Preheat the oven to 400°F (200°C). Place the halved red bell peppers on a baking sheet, cut side down. Roast in the preheated oven for about 20-25 minutes or until the skins are charred.

Remove the peppers from the oven and place them in a bowl. Cover the bowl with plastic wrap and let the peppers steam for about 10 minutes. Peel off the skins and chop the roasted peppers.

In a large pot, heat olive oil over medium heat. Add the chopped onion and cook until softened, about 5 minutes.

Add the minced garlic and cook for an additional 1-2 minutes until fragrant.

Pour in the whole peeled tomatoes (with their juices) and roasted red peppers. Break apart the tomatoes with a spoon or spatula.

Add the vegetable or chicken broth, dried basil, dried oregano, salt, and pepper. Bring the mixture to a boil, then reduce the heat to low and let it simmer for about 15-20 minutes.

Use an immersion blender to blend the soup until smooth. Alternatively, transfer the soup in batches to a blender, blend, and return it to the pot.

Stir in the heavy cream if using, and let the soup simmer for an additional 5 minutes.

Taste and adjust the seasoning if necessary.

Ladle the roasted red pepper and tomato soup into bowls, garnish with fresh basil leaves, and serve hot with croutons on top.

This vibrant and rich soup is perfect for a cozy winter evening. Enjoy its bold flavors and creamy texture with your favorite crusty bread or a side salad!

**Chicken and Wild Rice Soup**

Ingredients:

- 1 cup wild rice blend
- 1 pound (about 2 cups) boneless, skinless chicken breasts, cooked and shredded
- 3 tablespoons unsalted butter
- 1 onion, chopped
- 2 carrots, peeled and diced
- 2 celery stalks, diced
- 3 cloves garlic, minced
- 1/4 cup all-purpose flour
- 6 cups chicken broth
- 1 teaspoon dried thyme
- 1 teaspoon dried rosemary
- Salt and pepper to taste
- 1 cup mushrooms, sliced
- 1 cup frozen peas
- 1 cup milk or half-and-half
- Fresh parsley, chopped (for garnish)

Instructions:

Cook the wild rice blend according to the package instructions. Set aside.
In a large pot, melt the butter over medium heat. Add the chopped onion, carrots, and celery. Sauté until the vegetables are softened, about 5-7 minutes.
Add the minced garlic and cook for an additional 1-2 minutes until fragrant.
Stir in the all-purpose flour, coating the vegetables, and cook for 1-2 minutes to remove the raw taste of the flour.
Gradually whisk in the chicken broth, ensuring there are no lumps. Bring the mixture to a simmer.
Add the cooked and shredded chicken, dried thyme, dried rosemary, salt, and pepper to the pot. Let it simmer for about 15 minutes.
Add the sliced mushrooms, frozen peas, and cooked wild rice to the soup. Continue simmering for an additional 10-15 minutes.
Pour in the milk or half-and-half, and let the soup simmer for an additional 5 minutes.
Taste and adjust the seasoning if necessary.

Ladle the chicken and wild rice soup into bowls, garnish with chopped fresh parsley, and serve hot.

This hearty and creamy soup is a complete and satisfying meal. Enjoy it with some crusty bread or crackers for an extra touch!

**Italian Wedding Soup**

Ingredients:

*For Meatballs:*

- 1/2 pound ground beef
- 1/2 pound ground pork
- 1/2 cup breadcrumbs
- 1/4 cup grated Parmesan cheese
- 1/4 cup chopped fresh parsley
- 1 clove garlic, minced
- 1 large egg
- Salt and pepper to taste

*For Soup:*

- 1 tablespoon olive oil
- 1 onion, chopped
- 2 carrots, peeled and sliced
- 2 celery stalks, sliced
- 3 cloves garlic, minced
- 8 cups chicken broth
- 1 teaspoon dried oregano
- 1 teaspoon dried basil
- Salt and pepper to taste
- 1 cup small pasta (such as orzo or acini di pepe)
- 4 cups baby spinach or kale, chopped
- 1/2 cup grated Parmesan cheese (for serving)

Instructions:

Prepare Meatballs:
- In a bowl, combine ground beef, ground pork, breadcrumbs, grated Parmesan, chopped parsley, minced garlic, egg, salt, and pepper.
- Form small meatballs, about 1 inch in diameter.
- Place them on a baking sheet lined with parchment paper.
- Bake in a preheated oven at 375°F (190°C) for about 15-20 minutes or until cooked through.

Prepare Soup:
- In a large pot, heat olive oil over medium heat. Add chopped onion, sliced carrots, and sliced celery. Sauté until vegetables are softened, about 5-7 minutes.
- Add minced garlic and cook for an additional 1-2 minutes.
- Pour in the chicken broth, dried oregano, and dried basil. Season with salt and pepper to taste.
- Bring the soup to a simmer and add the cooked meatballs.
- Cook for 10-15 minutes to allow the flavors to meld.

Add Pasta and Greens:
- Add the small pasta to the soup and cook according to the package instructions until al dente.
- Stir in the chopped baby spinach or kale and cook until wilted.

Serve:
- Ladle the Italian Wedding Soup into bowls.
- Sprinkle each serving with grated Parmesan cheese.

This soup is a comforting and flavorful option, perfect for warming up on cold days. Enjoy this Italian classic with crusty bread on the side!

**Corn Chowder**

Ingredients:

- 4 cups fresh or frozen corn kernels (about 6-8 ears of corn)
- 4 slices bacon, chopped
- 1 onion, finely chopped
- 2 celery stalks, diced
- 1 red bell pepper, diced
- 3 tablespoons all-purpose flour
- 4 cups chicken or vegetable broth
- 2 large potatoes, peeled and diced
- 1 teaspoon dried thyme
- 1 teaspoon smoked paprika
- Salt and pepper to taste
- 2 cups whole milk or half-and-half
- Fresh chives, chopped (for garnish)
- Shredded cheddar cheese (for garnish)

Instructions:

Cook Bacon and Vegetables:
- In a large pot, cook the chopped bacon over medium heat until crispy.
- Add the chopped onion, diced celery, and diced red bell pepper to the pot. Sauté until the vegetables are softened, about 5-7 minutes.

Make Roux:
- Sprinkle flour over the bacon and vegetable mixture. Stir well to combine and cook for an additional 2 minutes to create a roux.

Add Broth and Potatoes:
- Gradually pour in the chicken or vegetable broth, stirring continuously to avoid lumps.
- Add diced potatoes, dried thyme, smoked paprika, salt, and pepper. Bring the mixture to a simmer and cook until the potatoes are tender, about 15-20 minutes.

Add Corn and Milk:
- Add the fresh or frozen corn kernels to the soup. If using fresh corn, scrape the cobs to extract any remaining pulp and juices.
- Pour in the whole milk or half-and-half and let the soup simmer for an additional 10-15 minutes.

Adjust Seasoning and Serve:
- Taste the chowder and adjust the seasoning with salt and pepper as needed.
- Ladle the corn chowder into bowls, garnish with chopped fresh chives and shredded cheddar cheese.

This Corn Chowder is a delightful blend of flavors and textures, making it a comforting choice for a winter meal. Enjoy it with a slice of crusty bread or crackers!

**Spicy Pumpkin Soup**

Ingredients:

- 2 tablespoons olive oil
- 1 onion, chopped
- 3 cloves garlic, minced
- 1 teaspoon ground cumin
- 1 teaspoon ground coriander
- 1/2 teaspoon smoked paprika
- 1/4 teaspoon cayenne pepper (adjust to taste)
- 4 cups pumpkin puree (canned or homemade)
- 4 cups vegetable or chicken broth
- 1 can (14 ounces) coconut milk
- Salt and pepper to taste
- Juice of 1 lime
- Fresh cilantro, chopped (for garnish)
- Toasted pumpkin seeds (for garnish)

Instructions:

Sauté Aromatics:
- In a large pot, heat olive oil over medium heat. Add the chopped onion and cook until softened, about 5-7 minutes.
- Add minced garlic and continue to cook for an additional 1-2 minutes until fragrant.

Add Spices:
- Stir in ground cumin, ground coriander, smoked paprika, and cayenne pepper. Cook for another 1-2 minutes to toast the spices.

Combine Pumpkin and Broth:
- Add pumpkin puree and vegetable or chicken broth to the pot. Stir well to combine.

Simmer:
- Bring the mixture to a simmer and let it cook for about 15-20 minutes, allowing the flavors to meld.

Blend and Add Coconut Milk:
- Use an immersion blender to blend the soup until smooth. Alternatively, transfer the soup in batches to a blender, blend, and return it to the pot.

- Stir in the coconut milk and let the soup simmer for an additional 5-10 minutes.

Season and Finish:
- Season the soup with salt and pepper to taste.
- Squeeze in the lime juice and stir well.

Serve:
- Ladle the spicy pumpkin soup into bowls.
- Garnish with chopped fresh cilantro and toasted pumpkin seeds.

This Spicy Pumpkin Soup offers a balance of heat and sweetness, making it a comforting and unique dish. Enjoy it with a dollop of sour cream or a swirl of coconut milk if desired!

**Mushroom and Barley Soup**

Ingredients:

- 1 cup pearl barley, rinsed
- 2 tablespoons olive oil
- 1 onion, chopped
- 2 carrots, peeled and diced
- 2 celery stalks, diced
- 3 cloves garlic, minced
- 1 pound (about 500g) mushrooms, sliced (use a mix of varieties like cremini, shiitake, and button mushrooms)
- 1 teaspoon dried thyme
- 1 teaspoon dried rosemary
- 8 cups vegetable or beef broth
- Salt and pepper to taste
- 1 bay leaf
- 1/4 cup soy sauce
- Fresh parsley, chopped (for garnish)

Instructions:

Prepare Barley:
- In a separate pot, cook the rinsed pearl barley according to the package instructions. Set aside.

Sauté Vegetables:
- In a large pot, heat olive oil over medium heat. Add chopped onion, diced carrots, and diced celery. Sauté until the vegetables are softened, about 5-7 minutes.

Add Mushrooms:
- Add minced garlic and sliced mushrooms to the pot. Cook until the mushrooms release their moisture and become golden brown.

Season and Simmer:
- Stir in dried thyme and dried rosemary. Season with salt and pepper to taste.
- Pour in the vegetable or beef broth, add the bay leaf, and bring the mixture to a simmer. Let it simmer for about 15-20 minutes.

Incorporate Barley:
- Add the cooked barley to the soup and stir well.

Enhance Flavor:
- Pour in soy sauce to enhance the umami flavor. Adjust the seasoning if necessary.

Finish and Serve:
- Allow the soup to simmer for an additional 5-10 minutes.
- Remove the bay leaf before serving.
- Ladle the mushroom and barley soup into bowls, garnish with chopped fresh parsley, and serve hot.

This Mushroom and Barley Soup is a wholesome and satisfying dish. Enjoy it with a slice of crusty bread or as part of a hearty winter meal!

**Turkey and Vegetable Soup**

Ingredients:

- 2 tablespoons olive oil
- 1 onion, chopped
- 2 carrots, peeled and diced
- 2 celery stalks, diced
- 3 cloves garlic, minced
- 4 cups cooked turkey, shredded or diced
- 8 cups turkey or chicken broth
- 1 can (14 ounces) diced tomatoes
- 1 cup green beans, chopped
- 1 cup corn kernels (fresh, frozen, or canned)
- 1 cup peas (fresh or frozen)
- 1 teaspoon dried thyme
- 1 teaspoon dried rosemary
- Salt and pepper to taste
- 1 bay leaf
- 1 cup pasta (such as small shells or rotini)
- Fresh parsley, chopped (for garnish)

Instructions:

Sauté Vegetables:
- In a large pot, heat olive oil over medium heat. Add chopped onion, diced carrots, and diced celery. Sauté until the vegetables are softened, about 5-7 minutes.

Add Turkey:
- Add minced garlic and cooked turkey to the pot. Stir well to combine.

Combine Broth and Tomatoes:
- Pour in the turkey or chicken broth and add the diced tomatoes (with their juices). Stir to combine.

Add Vegetables and Seasonings:
- Add chopped green beans, corn kernels, peas, dried thyme, dried rosemary, salt, pepper, and the bay leaf. Mix well.

Simmer:
- Bring the soup to a simmer and let it cook for about 15-20 minutes to allow the flavors to meld.

Cook Pasta:
- In a separate pot, cook the pasta according to the package instructions. Drain and set aside.

Combine Pasta and Finish Soup:
- Add the cooked pasta to the soup and stir well.

Adjust Seasoning and Serve:
- Taste and adjust the seasoning if necessary.
- Remove the bay leaf before serving.
- Ladle the turkey and vegetable soup into bowls, garnish with chopped fresh parsley, and serve hot.

This Turkey and Vegetable Soup is a fantastic way to use leftover turkey and create a comforting and nutritious meal. Enjoy it with a side of crusty bread for a complete experience!

**Ham and Potato Chowder**

Ingredients:

- 3 cups potatoes, peeled and diced
- 1/2 cup onion, chopped
- 1/2 cup celery, chopped
- 1/2 cup carrots, diced
- 3 tablespoons butter
- 3 tablespoons all-purpose flour
- 3 cups ham, cooked and diced
- 4 cups chicken broth
- 1 teaspoon dried thyme
- 1 teaspoon dried rosemary
- Salt and pepper to taste
- 2 cups milk
- 1 cup sharp cheddar cheese, shredded
- Green onions, chopped (for garnish)

Instructions:

Prepare Vegetables:
- In a large pot, combine diced potatoes, chopped onion, diced celery, and diced carrots.

Make Roux:
- In a separate saucepan, melt butter over medium heat. Stir in flour to create a roux. Cook for 1-2 minutes to remove the raw taste of the flour.

Add Ham and Broth:
- Add diced ham to the pot with vegetables. Pour in the chicken broth and bring the mixture to a boil.

Combine Ingredients:
- Reduce the heat to a simmer. Add dried thyme, dried rosemary, salt, and pepper. Stir to combine.

Cook Vegetables:
- Let the soup simmer until the vegetables are tender, about 15-20 minutes.

Add Milk and Cheese:
- Pour in the milk and add shredded cheddar cheese. Stir until the cheese is melted and the soup is creamy.

Adjust Seasoning:

- Taste the chowder and adjust the seasoning with salt and pepper as needed.

Serve:
- Ladle the ham and potato chowder into bowls.
- Garnish with chopped green onions.

This Ham and Potato Chowder is a delicious and comforting way to enjoy leftover ham. Serve it with a side of crusty bread for a complete and satisfying meal!

**Broccoli Cheddar Soup**

Ingredients:

- 1/4 cup unsalted butter
- 1 onion, chopped
- 2 carrots, peeled and diced
- 2 celery stalks, diced
- 3 cups broccoli florets, chopped
- 1/4 cup all-purpose flour
- 4 cups chicken or vegetable broth
- 2 cups milk
- 2 cups sharp cheddar cheese, shredded
- Salt and pepper to taste
- 1/4 teaspoon nutmeg (optional)
- 1 cup half-and-half or heavy cream (optional, for extra creaminess)
- Croutons or additional shredded cheddar for garnish

Instructions:

Sauté Vegetables:
- In a large pot, melt butter over medium heat. Add chopped onion, diced carrots, and diced celery. Cook until the vegetables are softened, about 5-7 minutes.

Add Broccoli:
- Add chopped broccoli florets to the pot and cook for an additional 3-4 minutes.

Make Roux:
- Sprinkle flour over the vegetables and stir to combine, creating a roux. Cook for 1-2 minutes to remove the raw taste of the flour.

Add Broth and Milk:
- Gradually pour in the chicken or vegetable broth, stirring continuously to avoid lumps.
- Add milk to the pot and bring the mixture to a simmer.

Simmer:
- Let the soup simmer until the broccoli is tender, about 15-20 minutes.

Blend (Optional):

- For a smoother texture, use an immersion blender to blend the soup until desired consistency. Alternatively, transfer a portion of the soup to a blender, blend, and return it to the pot.

Add Cheese:
- Stir in shredded cheddar cheese until melted and incorporated into the soup.

Season:
- Season with salt and pepper to taste. Add nutmeg if desired.

Add Cream (Optional):
- For extra creaminess, stir in half-and-half or heavy cream.

Serve:
- Ladle the broccoli cheddar soup into bowls.
- Garnish with croutons or additional shredded cheddar cheese.

This Broccoli Cheddar Soup is rich, creamy, and full of flavor. Enjoy it as a comforting meal on its own or paired with a slice of crusty bread!

**Cabbage Roll Soup**

Ingredients:

- 1 pound ground beef
- 1 onion, chopped
- 2 cloves garlic, minced
- 1 small cabbage, chopped
- 2 carrots, peeled and diced
- 1 can (14 ounces) diced tomatoes
- 1 can (8 ounces) tomato sauce
- 6 cups beef broth
- 1 cup cooked rice
- 1 teaspoon dried thyme
- 1 teaspoon dried oregano
- Salt and pepper to taste
- 1 bay leaf
- Fresh parsley, chopped (for garnish)
- Sour cream (optional, for serving)

Instructions:

Brown Ground Beef:
- In a large pot, brown the ground beef over medium-high heat. Drain excess fat if needed.

Sauté Vegetables:
- Add chopped onion and minced garlic to the pot. Sauté until the onion is translucent.

Add Cabbage and Carrots:
- Stir in chopped cabbage and diced carrots. Cook for 5-7 minutes or until the cabbage starts to wilt.

Add Tomatoes and Sauce:
- Add diced tomatoes and tomato sauce to the pot. Stir to combine.

Pour in Beef Broth:
- Pour in the beef broth, and add dried thyme, dried oregano, salt, pepper, and the bay leaf. Bring the mixture to a simmer.

Simmer:
- Let the soup simmer for about 20-25 minutes or until the cabbage and carrots are tender.

Add Cooked Rice:
- Stir in the cooked rice and let the soup simmer for an additional 5 minutes.

Adjust Seasoning:
- Taste and adjust the seasoning as needed.

Serve:
- Ladle the cabbage roll soup into bowls.
- Garnish with chopped fresh parsley and serve hot.
- Optionally, serve with a dollop of sour cream.

This Cabbage Roll Soup captures all the delicious flavors of cabbage rolls in a convenient and comforting bowl. Enjoy it with a side of crusty bread for a hearty and satisfying meal!

**Moroccan Chickpea Soup**

Ingredients:

- 2 tablespoons olive oil
- 1 onion, chopped
- 2 carrots, peeled and diced
- 2 celery stalks, diced
- 3 cloves garlic, minced
- 1 teaspoon ground cumin
- 1 teaspoon ground coriander
- 1 teaspoon ground turmeric
- 1/2 teaspoon ground cinnamon
- 1/4 teaspoon cayenne pepper (adjust to taste)
- 1 can (15 ounces) chickpeas, drained and rinsed
- 1 can (14 ounces) diced tomatoes
- 4 cups vegetable broth
- 1 cup red lentils, rinsed
- 1 bay leaf
- Salt and pepper to taste
- Juice of 1 lemon
- Fresh cilantro, chopped (for garnish)
- Greek yogurt or sour cream (optional, for serving)

Instructions:

Sauté Aromatics:
- In a large pot, heat olive oil over medium heat. Add chopped onion, diced carrots, and diced celery. Sauté until the vegetables are softened, about 5-7 minutes.

Add Spices:
- Add minced garlic, ground cumin, ground coriander, ground turmeric, ground cinnamon, and cayenne pepper. Stir well and cook for an additional 2 minutes to toast the spices.

Combine Chickpeas and Tomatoes:
- Add chickpeas and diced tomatoes (with their juices) to the pot. Stir to combine.

Pour in Broth:

- Pour in the vegetable broth and add red lentils. Add the bay leaf. Bring the mixture to a simmer.

Simmer:
- Let the soup simmer for about 20-25 minutes, or until the lentils are tender.

Season:
- Season the soup with salt and pepper to taste.

Add Lemon Juice:
- Squeeze in the juice of one lemon. Adjust the acidity to your liking.

Serve:
- Ladle the Moroccan Chickpea Soup into bowls.
- Garnish with chopped fresh cilantro.
- Optionally, serve with a dollop of Greek yogurt or sour cream.

This Moroccan Chickpea Soup is a delightful blend of spices and textures. Enjoy the warm and aromatic flavors, and feel free to customize the spice levels to suit your taste preferences!

**Chili con Carne**

Ingredients:

- 1.5 pounds ground beef
- 1 large onion, finely chopped
- 3 cloves garlic, minced
- 1 bell pepper, diced
- 2 cans (15 ounces each) kidney beans, drained and rinsed
- 1 can (28 ounces) crushed tomatoes
- 1 can (6 ounces) tomato paste
- 2 cups beef broth
- 2 tablespoons chili powder
- 1 teaspoon ground cumin
- 1 teaspoon paprika
- 1/2 teaspoon cayenne pepper (adjust to taste)
- 1 teaspoon dried oregano
- Salt and pepper to taste
- 1-2 tablespoons vegetable oil (for cooking)
- Optional toppings: shredded cheese, sour cream, chopped green onions, cilantro

Instructions:

Cook Ground Beef:
- In a large pot or Dutch oven, heat vegetable oil over medium heat. Add ground beef and cook until browned, breaking it apart with a spoon as it cooks.

Sauté Aromatics:
- Add chopped onion, minced garlic, and diced bell pepper to the pot. Sauté until the vegetables are softened.

Add Tomatoes and Paste:
- Stir in crushed tomatoes and tomato paste. Mix well to combine.

Combine Beans:
- Add drained and rinsed kidney beans to the pot.

Pour in Broth:
- Pour in beef broth and stir to incorporate all the ingredients.

Season:
- Add chili powder, ground cumin, paprika, cayenne pepper, dried oregano, salt, and pepper. Adjust the seasoning to your taste.

Simmer:
- Bring the chili to a simmer. Reduce the heat to low, cover, and let it simmer for at least 30 minutes to allow the flavors to meld. You can simmer for longer if you have the time.

Adjust Consistency:
- If the chili is too thick, you can add more beef broth to achieve your desired consistency.

Serve:
- Ladle the Chili con Carne into bowls.
- Garnish with shredded cheese, sour cream, chopped green onions, cilantro, or your favorite toppings.

This Chili con Carne is a classic comfort food that's perfect for serving on its own or with some crusty bread or rice. Enjoy the rich and robust flavors!

**Chicken Tortilla Soup**

Ingredients:

- 1 tablespoon olive oil
- 1 onion, chopped
- 3 cloves garlic, minced
- 1 jalapeño, seeded and finely chopped
- 1 teaspoon ground cumin
- 1 teaspoon chili powder
- 1 teaspoon paprika
- 1 can (14 ounces) diced tomatoes
- 1 can (4 ounces) diced green chilies
- 6 cups chicken broth
- 1 pound boneless, skinless chicken breasts or thighs, cooked and shredded
- 1 cup corn kernels (fresh, frozen, or canned)
- 1 can (15 ounces) black beans, drained and rinsed
- Salt and pepper to taste
- Juice of 1 lime
- Fresh cilantro, chopped (for garnish)
- Tortilla strips or chips (for serving)
- Avocado slices (for serving)
- Shredded cheese (cheddar or Mexican blend, for serving)
- Sour cream (optional, for serving)

Instructions:

Sauté Aromatics:
- In a large pot, heat olive oil over medium heat. Add chopped onion, minced garlic, and jalapeño. Sauté until the vegetables are softened.

Add Spices:
- Stir in ground cumin, chili powder, and paprika. Cook for an additional 1-2 minutes to toast the spices.

Combine Tomatoes and Chilies:
- Add diced tomatoes and diced green chilies to the pot. Mix well.

Pour in Broth:
- Pour in the chicken broth and bring the mixture to a simmer.

Add Chicken, Corn, and Beans:

- Add shredded chicken, corn kernels, and black beans to the pot. Season with salt and pepper to taste.

Simmer:
- Let the soup simmer for about 15-20 minutes to allow the flavors to meld.

Finish and Season:
- Squeeze in the juice of one lime. Taste and adjust the seasoning if necessary.

Serve:
- Ladle the Chicken Tortilla Soup into bowls.
- Garnish with fresh cilantro, tortilla strips or chips, avocado slices, shredded cheese, and a dollop of sour cream if desired.

This Chicken Tortilla Soup is a delightful and satisfying meal. Enjoy the combination of flavors and textures, and feel free to customize the toppings according to your preferences!

**Sweet Potato and Black Bean Soup**

Ingredients:

- 2 tablespoons olive oil
- 1 onion, chopped
- 3 cloves garlic, minced
- 2 sweet potatoes, peeled and diced
- 2 carrots, peeled and diced
- 1 red bell pepper, diced
- 1 teaspoon ground cumin
- 1 teaspoon chili powder
- 1/2 teaspoon ground coriander
- 1/4 teaspoon cayenne pepper (adjust to taste)
- 2 cans (15 ounces each) black beans, drained and rinsed
- 1 can (14 ounces) diced tomatoes
- 6 cups vegetable broth
- Salt and pepper to taste
- Juice of 1 lime
- Fresh cilantro, chopped (for garnish)
- Avocado slices (for garnish)
- Greek yogurt or sour cream (optional, for serving)

Instructions:

Sauté Aromatics:
- In a large pot, heat olive oil over medium heat. Add chopped onion and sauté until softened.

Add Vegetables:
- Stir in minced garlic, diced sweet potatoes, diced carrots, and diced red bell pepper. Cook for 5-7 minutes until the vegetables start to soften.

Season with Spices:
- Add ground cumin, chili powder, ground coriander, and cayenne pepper. Stir well to coat the vegetables in the spices.

Combine Black Beans and Tomatoes:
- Add drained and rinsed black beans and diced tomatoes (with their juices) to the pot. Mix well.

Pour in Broth:
- Pour in the vegetable broth and bring the mixture to a simmer.

Simmer:
- Let the soup simmer for about 15-20 minutes or until the sweet potatoes are tender.

Season and Finish:
- Season the soup with salt and pepper to taste.
- Squeeze in the juice of one lime and stir well.

Serve:
- Ladle the Sweet Potato and Black Bean Soup into bowls.
- Garnish with chopped fresh cilantro, avocado slices, and a dollop of Greek yogurt or sour cream if desired.

This Sweet Potato and Black Bean Soup is a hearty and nutrient-rich dish. Enjoy the vibrant colors and flavors, and feel free to adjust the spice levels and toppings to suit your taste!

**Lemon Chicken Orzo Soup**

Ingredients:

- 1 tablespoon olive oil
- 1 onion, chopped
- 2 carrots, peeled and diced
- 2 celery stalks, diced
- 3 cloves garlic, minced
- 1 pound boneless, skinless chicken breasts, cut into small pieces
- 8 cups chicken broth
- 1 cup orzo pasta
- 2 teaspoons dried thyme
- Salt and pepper to taste
- Juice of 2 lemons
- Zest of 1 lemon
- 1 cup baby spinach or kale, chopped
- Fresh parsley, chopped (for garnish)

Instructions:

Sauté Aromatics:
- In a large pot, heat olive oil over medium heat. Add chopped onion, diced carrots, and diced celery. Sauté until the vegetables are softened, about 5-7 minutes.

Add Chicken:
- Add minced garlic and cut chicken pieces to the pot. Cook until the chicken is no longer pink.

Pour in Broth:
- Pour in chicken broth and bring the mixture to a simmer.

Add Orzo and Thyme:
- Add orzo pasta and dried thyme to the pot. Season with salt and pepper to taste.

Simmer:
- Let the soup simmer for about 10-12 minutes or until the orzo is cooked and the chicken is fully cooked through.

Add Lemon Juice and Zest:
- Squeeze in the juice of two lemons and add the zest of one lemon to the pot. Adjust the lemony flavor to your liking.

Add Greens:
- Stir in chopped baby spinach or kale and let it wilt into the soup.

Adjust Seasoning:
- Taste and adjust the seasoning with salt and pepper if needed.

Serve:
- Ladle the Lemon Chicken Orzo Soup into bowls.
- Garnish with fresh parsley.

This Lemon Chicken Orzo Soup is a comforting and citrusy option. Enjoy its light and flavorful profile, perfect for a warming meal on a cool day!

**Creamy Cauliflower Soup**

Ingredients:

- 1 large cauliflower, chopped into florets
- 1 onion, chopped
- 2 cloves garlic, minced
- 2 tablespoons olive oil
- 4 cups vegetable broth
- 1 cup milk (whole milk or unsweetened almond milk)
- 1/2 cup heavy cream
- Salt and pepper to taste
- 1/2 teaspoon nutmeg (optional)
- Fresh chives or parsley, chopped (for garnish)

Instructions:

Sauté Vegetables:
- In a large pot, heat olive oil over medium heat. Add chopped onion and minced garlic. Sauté until the onion is translucent.

Add Cauliflower:
- Add the chopped cauliflower florets to the pot. Cook for 5-7 minutes until slightly softened.

Pour in Broth:
- Pour in the vegetable broth, ensuring the cauliflower is mostly covered. Bring the mixture to a simmer.

Simmer:
- Let the soup simmer for about 15-20 minutes or until the cauliflower is tender.

Blend:
- Use an immersion blender to puree the soup until smooth. Alternatively, transfer the soup in batches to a blender and blend until smooth. Be cautious when blending hot liquids.

Add Milk and Cream:
- Pour in the milk and heavy cream. Stir well to combine.

Season:
- Season the soup with salt, pepper, and nutmeg (if using). Adjust the seasoning to your taste.

Heat Through:

- Let the soup heat through, but do not boil once the dairy is added.

Serve:
- Ladle the Creamy Cauliflower Soup into bowls.
- Garnish with chopped fresh chives or parsley.

This Creamy Cauliflower Soup is a comforting and satisfying option, perfect for a cozy meal. Enjoy it with a slice of crusty bread or as a light starter for dinner!

**Sausage and Kale Soup**

Ingredients:

- 1 pound Italian sausage, casings removed
- 1 onion, chopped
- 3 cloves garlic, minced
- 1 carrot, peeled and diced
- 2 celery stalks, diced
- 1 teaspoon dried thyme
- 1 teaspoon dried rosemary
- 1 bay leaf
- 6 cups chicken broth
- 1 can (14 ounces) diced tomatoes
- 2 cups potatoes, peeled and diced
- 4 cups kale, stems removed and chopped
- Salt and pepper to taste
- Red pepper flakes (optional, for heat)
- Grated Parmesan cheese (for serving)

Instructions:

Brown Sausage:
- In a large pot, brown the Italian sausage over medium heat, breaking it apart with a spoon as it cooks. Once browned, remove any excess fat.

Sauté Aromatics:
- Add chopped onion, minced garlic, diced carrot, and diced celery to the pot. Sauté until the vegetables are softened.

Season:
- Stir in dried thyme, dried rosemary, and the bay leaf. Season with salt and pepper to taste. Add red pepper flakes if you like a bit of heat.

Add Broth and Tomatoes:
- Pour in the chicken broth and add diced tomatoes (with their juices). Stir well.

Incorporate Potatoes and Kale:
- Add diced potatoes and chopped kale to the pot. Stir to combine.

Simmer:

- Bring the soup to a simmer and let it cook for about 15-20 minutes, or until the potatoes are tender and the kale is wilted.

Adjust Seasoning:
- Taste and adjust the seasoning if necessary. Remove the bay leaf.

Serve:
- Ladle the Sausage and Kale Soup into bowls.
- Sprinkle with grated Parmesan cheese before serving.

This Sausage and Kale Soup is a hearty and satisfying meal, perfect for a comforting dinner. Enjoy it with a slice of crusty bread or on its own!

**Coconut Curry Chicken Soup**

Ingredients:

- 1 tablespoon vegetable oil
- 1 onion, chopped
- 3 cloves garlic, minced
- 1 tablespoon ginger, grated
- 2 tablespoons red curry paste
- 1 pound boneless, skinless chicken breasts, thinly sliced
- 4 cups chicken broth
- 1 can (14 ounces) coconut milk
- 1 red bell pepper, thinly sliced
- 1 carrot, julienned
- 1 zucchini, julienned
- 1 tablespoon fish sauce
- 1 tablespoon soy sauce
- 1 tablespoon brown sugar
- Juice of 1 lime
- Salt and pepper to taste
- Fresh cilantro, chopped (for garnish)
- Cooked rice or rice noodles (optional, for serving)

Instructions:

Sauté Aromatics:
- In a large pot, heat vegetable oil over medium heat. Add chopped onion and sauté until softened.

Add Garlic, Ginger, and Curry Paste:
- Add minced garlic and grated ginger to the pot. Stir in red curry paste and cook for 1-2 minutes to release the flavors.

Cook Chicken:
- Add thinly sliced chicken breasts to the pot and cook until they are no longer pink.

Pour in Broth and Coconut Milk:
- Pour in chicken broth and coconut milk. Bring the mixture to a simmer.

Add Vegetables:

- Add thinly sliced red bell pepper, julienned carrot, and julienned zucchini to the pot. Cook for about 5-7 minutes until the vegetables are tender but still vibrant.

Season:
- Stir in fish sauce, soy sauce, brown sugar, and the juice of one lime. Season with salt and pepper to taste. Adjust the seasoning as needed.

Simmer:
- Let the soup simmer for an additional 5-10 minutes to allow the flavors to meld.

Serve:
- Ladle the Coconut Curry Chicken Soup into bowls.
- Garnish with chopped fresh cilantro.
- Optionally, serve over cooked rice or rice noodles.

This Coconut Curry Chicken Soup is a comforting and exotic dish with a perfect balance of flavors. Enjoy the warmth and richness of this soup as a delightful meal!

**Quinoa Vegetable Soup**

Ingredients:

- 1 cup quinoa, rinsed
- 1 tablespoon olive oil
- 1 onion, chopped
- 3 cloves garlic, minced
- 2 carrots, peeled and diced
- 2 celery stalks, diced
- 1 bell pepper, diced
- 1 zucchini, diced
- 1 can (14 ounces) diced tomatoes
- 8 cups vegetable broth
- 1 teaspoon dried thyme
- 1 teaspoon dried rosemary
- 1 teaspoon ground cumin
- Salt and pepper to taste
- 2 cups kale or spinach, chopped
- Juice of 1 lemon
- Fresh parsley, chopped (for garnish)

Instructions:

Cook Quinoa:
- In a separate pot, cook quinoa according to package instructions. Set aside.

Sauté Vegetables:
- In a large pot, heat olive oil over medium heat. Add chopped onion, minced garlic, diced carrots, diced celery, diced bell pepper, and diced zucchini. Sauté until the vegetables are softened.

Add Tomatoes and Broth:
- Stir in diced tomatoes (with their juices) and pour in vegetable broth. Bring the mixture to a simmer.

Season:
- Add dried thyme, dried rosemary, ground cumin, salt, and pepper. Adjust the seasoning to your taste.

Simmer:

- Let the soup simmer for about 15-20 minutes, allowing the flavors to meld and the vegetables to become tender.

Add Cooked Quinoa:
- Add the cooked quinoa to the pot and stir well.

Incorporate Greens and Lemon Juice:
- Stir in chopped kale or spinach and squeeze in the juice of one lemon. Cook until the greens are wilted.

Adjust Seasoning:
- Taste and adjust the seasoning if necessary.

Serve:
- Ladle the Quinoa Vegetable Soup into bowls.
- Garnish with chopped fresh parsley.

This Quinoa Vegetable Soup is a nutritious and filling option, perfect for a wholesome meal. Enjoy the blend of quinoa, vegetables, and aromatic herbs in this comforting soup!

**Three-Bean Chili**

Ingredients:

- 1 tablespoon olive oil
- 1 onion, chopped
- 3 cloves garlic, minced
- 1 bell pepper, diced
- 2 carrots, peeled and diced
- 2 celery stalks, diced
- 1 zucchini, diced
- 1 can (15 ounces) black beans, drained and rinsed
- 1 can (15 ounces) kidney beans, drained and rinsed
- 1 can (15 ounces) pinto beans, drained and rinsed
- 1 can (14 ounces) diced tomatoes
- 1 can (6 ounces) tomato paste
- 4 cups vegetable broth
- 2 teaspoons chili powder
- 1 teaspoon ground cumin
- 1 teaspoon smoked paprika
- 1/2 teaspoon cayenne pepper (adjust to taste)
- Salt and pepper to taste
- 1 cup frozen corn kernels
- Juice of 1 lime
- Fresh cilantro, chopped (for garnish)
- Avocado slices (for garnish)
- Shredded cheese (cheddar or Mexican blend, for serving)
- Sour cream (optional, for serving)

Instructions:

Sauté Aromatics:
- In a large pot, heat olive oil over medium heat. Add chopped onion, minced garlic, diced bell pepper, diced carrots, and diced celery. Sauté until the vegetables are softened.

Add Zucchini and Beans:
- Stir in diced zucchini, black beans, kidney beans, and pinto beans. Mix well.

Combine Tomatoes and Paste:
- Add diced tomatoes (with their juices) and tomato paste to the pot. Stir to combine.

Pour in Broth:
- Pour in vegetable broth and bring the mixture to a simmer.

Season:
- Add chili powder, ground cumin, smoked paprika, cayenne pepper, salt, and pepper. Adjust the seasoning to your taste.

Simmer:
- Let the chili simmer for about 20-25 minutes to allow the flavors to meld.

Add Corn and Lime Juice:
- Stir in frozen corn kernels and squeeze in the juice of one lime. Cook for an additional 5 minutes.

Adjust Seasoning:
- Taste and adjust the seasoning if necessary.

Serve:
- Ladle the Three-Bean Chili into bowls.
- Garnish with chopped fresh cilantro, avocado slices, shredded cheese, and a dollop of sour cream if desired.

This Three-Bean Chili is a wholesome and satisfying vegetarian option. Enjoy it on its own or serve it over rice or with a side of crusty bread!

**Cream of Asparagus Soup**

Ingredients:

- 2 pounds fresh asparagus, trimmed and chopped
- 3 tablespoons unsalted butter
- 1 onion, chopped
- 2 cloves garlic, minced
- 4 cups vegetable broth
- 1 potato, peeled and diced
- 1 cup heavy cream
- Salt and pepper to taste
- Pinch of nutmeg (optional)
- Lemon zest (optional, for garnish)
- Fresh chives or parsley, chopped (for garnish)

Instructions:

Sauté Vegetables:
- In a large pot, melt butter over medium heat. Add chopped onion and minced garlic. Sauté until the onion is translucent.

Add Asparagus:
- Add chopped asparagus to the pot and cook for 5-7 minutes, stirring occasionally.

Pour in Broth:
- Pour in vegetable broth and add diced potato. Bring the mixture to a simmer.

Simmer:
- Let the soup simmer for about 15-20 minutes or until the asparagus and potatoes are tender.

Blend:
- Use an immersion blender to puree the soup until smooth. Alternatively, transfer the soup in batches to a blender and blend until smooth. Be cautious when blending hot liquids.

Add Cream:
- Stir in heavy cream and continue to simmer for an additional 5 minutes.

Season:
- Season the soup with salt and pepper to taste. Add a pinch of nutmeg for additional flavor if desired.

Adjust Consistency:
- If the soup is too thick, you can add more vegetable broth or water to reach your desired consistency.

Serve:
- Ladle the Cream of Asparagus Soup into bowls.
- Garnish with a sprinkle of lemon zest and chopped fresh chives or parsley.

This Cream of Asparagus Soup is a creamy and luxurious option, perfect for a light lunch or as a starter for a special meal. Enjoy the vibrant flavors of asparagus in this delicious soup!

## Italian Sausage and Tortellini Soup

Ingredients:

- 1 tablespoon olive oil
- 1 pound Italian sausage, casings removed
- 1 onion, chopped
- 3 cloves garlic, minced
- 1 carrot, diced
- 1 celery stalk, diced
- 1 bell pepper, diced
- 6 cups chicken broth
- 1 can (14 ounces) diced tomatoes
- 1 can (6 ounces) tomato paste
- 1 teaspoon dried basil
- 1 teaspoon dried oregano
- 1/2 teaspoon dried thyme
- Salt and pepper to taste
- 1 package (about 9 ounces) refrigerated or frozen cheese tortellini
- 2 cups fresh spinach or kale, chopped
- Grated Parmesan cheese (for serving)
- Fresh basil, chopped (for garnish)

Instructions:

Brown Sausage:
- In a large pot, heat olive oil over medium heat. Add the Italian sausage, breaking it apart with a spoon as it cooks. Brown the sausage until cooked through. Remove any excess fat.

Sauté Vegetables:
- Add chopped onion, minced garlic, diced carrot, diced celery, and diced bell pepper to the pot. Sauté until the vegetables are softened.

Add Broth and Tomatoes:
- Pour in the chicken broth and add diced tomatoes (with their juices). Stir well.

Season:
- Stir in tomato paste, dried basil, dried oregano, dried thyme, salt, and pepper. Adjust the seasoning to your taste.

Simmer:

- Let the soup simmer for about 15-20 minutes to allow the flavors to meld.

Cook Tortellini:
- Add the cheese tortellini to the pot and cook according to the package instructions. Typically, it takes about 7-10 minutes for the tortellini to cook.

Add Spinach or Kale:
- Stir in the chopped fresh spinach or kale and let it wilt into the soup.

Adjust Seasoning:
- Taste and adjust the seasoning if necessary.

Serve:
- Ladle the Italian Sausage and Tortellini Soup into bowls.
- Garnish with grated Parmesan cheese and chopped fresh basil.

This Italian Sausage and Tortellini Soup is a satisfying and comforting meal. Enjoy the combination of flavors and textures in each spoonful!

**Ginger Carrot Soup**

Ingredients:

- 1 tablespoon olive oil
- 1 onion, chopped
- 2 pounds carrots, peeled and sliced
- 3 cloves garlic, minced
- 1 tablespoon fresh ginger, grated
- 4 cups vegetable broth
- 1 teaspoon ground cumin
- 1/2 teaspoon ground coriander
- 1/2 teaspoon ground turmeric
- Salt and pepper to taste
- 1 can (14 ounces) coconut milk
- Juice of 1 orange
- Zest of 1 orange (optional, for garnish)
- Fresh cilantro, chopped (for garnish)

Instructions:

Sauté Aromatics:
- In a large pot, heat olive oil over medium heat. Add chopped onion, sliced carrots, minced garlic, and grated ginger. Sauté until the vegetables are softened.

Pour in Broth:
- Pour in vegetable broth, ensuring that the carrots are mostly covered. Bring the mixture to a simmer.

Add Spices:
- Stir in ground cumin, ground coriander, ground turmeric, salt, and pepper. Mix well.

Simmer:
- Let the soup simmer for about 20-25 minutes or until the carrots are tender.

Blend:
- Use an immersion blender to puree the soup until smooth. Alternatively, transfer the soup in batches to a blender and blend until smooth. Be cautious when blending hot liquids.

Add Coconut Milk:
- Stir in coconut milk and let the soup simmer for an additional 5-7 minutes.

Add Orange Juice:
- Squeeze in the juice of one orange and stir well. Adjust the citrusy flavor to your liking.

Season:
- Taste and adjust the seasoning if necessary.

Serve:
- Ladle the Ginger Carrot Soup into bowls.
- Garnish with orange zest and chopped fresh cilantro.

This Ginger Carrot Soup is a flavorful and comforting option, perfect for a light lunch or as a starter for a special meal. Enjoy the warmth and brightness of this delicious soup!

**Beef Stew with Root Vegetables**

Ingredients:

- 2 pounds stewing beef, cut into bite-sized cubes
- 2 tablespoons vegetable oil
- 1 onion, chopped
- 3 cloves garlic, minced
- 4 cups beef broth
- 1 cup red wine (optional)
- 2 tablespoons tomato paste
- 2 bay leaves
- 1 teaspoon dried thyme
- Salt and pepper to taste
- 4 large carrots, peeled and cut into chunks
- 4 medium potatoes, peeled and cut into chunks
- 2 parsnips, peeled and cut into chunks
- 2 turnips, peeled and cut into chunks
- 1 cup frozen peas (optional)
- Chopped fresh parsley (for garnish)

Instructions:

Brown the Beef:
- In a large pot, heat vegetable oil over medium-high heat. Add the beef cubes and brown on all sides. Remove the beef and set aside.

Sauté Aromatics:
- In the same pot, add chopped onion and minced garlic. Sauté until the onion is translucent.

Deglaze the Pot:
- Pour in red wine (if using) to deglaze the pot, scraping up any browned bits from the bottom.

Add Broth and Tomato Paste:
- Return the browned beef to the pot. Add beef broth, tomato paste, bay leaves, dried thyme, salt, and pepper. Stir well.

Simmer:
- Bring the mixture to a simmer. Cover the pot and let it simmer for about 1.5 to 2 hours, or until the beef is tender.

Add Root Vegetables:

- Add carrots, potatoes, parsnips, and turnips to the pot. Continue simmering for an additional 30-45 minutes or until the vegetables are fork-tender.

Adjust Seasoning:
- Taste and adjust the seasoning if necessary. Remove the bay leaves.

Add Peas (Optional):
- If using frozen peas, add them to the pot in the last 5-10 minutes of cooking.

Serve:
- Ladle the Beef Stew with Root Vegetables into bowls.
- Garnish with chopped fresh parsley.

This Beef Stew with Root Vegetables is a wholesome and satisfying meal. Enjoy the rich flavors and tender beef, along with the hearty goodness of the root vegetables!

**Spinach and White Bean Soup**

Ingredients:

- 1 tablespoon olive oil
- 1 onion, chopped
- 3 cloves garlic, minced
- 2 carrots, peeled and diced
- 2 celery stalks, diced
- 1 teaspoon dried thyme
- 1 teaspoon dried rosemary
- 2 cans (15 ounces each) white beans (cannellini or Great Northern), drained and rinsed
- 6 cups vegetable broth
- 1 can (14 ounces) diced tomatoes
- 4 cups fresh spinach, chopped
- Salt and pepper to taste
- Juice of 1 lemon
- Grated Parmesan cheese (for serving)
- Crusty bread (for serving)

Instructions:

Sauté Aromatics:
- In a large pot, heat olive oil over medium heat. Add chopped onion, minced garlic, diced carrots, and diced celery. Sauté until the vegetables are softened.

Add Herbs and Beans:
- Stir in dried thyme, dried rosemary, and white beans. Mix well.

Pour in Broth:
- Add vegetable broth to the pot and bring the mixture to a simmer.

Incorporate Tomatoes:
- Add diced tomatoes (with their juices) to the pot. Stir to combine.

Simmer:
- Let the soup simmer for about 15-20 minutes to allow the flavors to meld.

Add Spinach:
- Stir in chopped fresh spinach and cook until wilted.

Season:
- Season the soup with salt and pepper to taste.

Finish with Lemon Juice:
- Squeeze in the juice of one lemon and stir well.

Serve:
- Ladle the Spinach and White Bean Soup into bowls.
- Garnish with grated Parmesan cheese.
- Serve with crusty bread on the side.

This Spinach and White Bean Soup is a light and nourishing option, perfect for a quick and healthy meal. Enjoy the combination of beans, vegetables, and greens in this delightful soup!

**Thai Tom Yum Soup**

Ingredients:

*For the Broth:*

- 4 cups chicken or vegetable broth
- 2 lemongrass stalks, bruised and chopped into 3-inch pieces
- 3 kaffir lime leaves, torn into pieces
- 3 slices galangal (or ginger if unavailable)
- 3 Thai bird's eye chilies, smashed (adjust according to spice preference)
- 2 cloves garlic, smashed
- 1 medium-sized tomato, sliced
- 1 small onion, sliced
- 1 tablespoon fish sauce (adjust to taste)
- 1 tablespoon soy sauce
- 1 teaspoon sugar

*Additional Ingredients:*

- 200g (7 oz) shrimp, peeled and deveined
- 200g (7 oz) mushrooms, sliced
- 1 cup cherry tomatoes, halved
- 200g (7 oz) firm tofu, cubed (optional)
- Fresh cilantro leaves, for garnish
- Lime wedges, for serving

Instructions:

Prepare the Broth:
- In a pot, combine the chicken or vegetable broth, lemongrass, kaffir lime leaves, galangal, Thai bird's eye chilies, garlic, tomato, and onion.
- Bring the broth to a simmer over medium heat. Let it simmer for about 15-20 minutes to infuse the flavors.

Strain the Broth:
- Strain the broth to remove the solid ingredients, leaving you with a clear and aromatic broth.

Add Additional Ingredients:

- Return the strained broth to the pot. Add fish sauce, soy sauce, and sugar. Adjust the seasoning to your taste.
- Add shrimp, mushrooms, cherry tomatoes, and tofu (if using). Cook until the shrimp turns pink and opaque.

Serve:
- Ladle the Tom Yum Soup into bowls.
- Garnish with fresh cilantro leaves.
- Serve with lime wedges on the side.

This Tom Yum Soup is a delightful balance of spicy, sour, and savory flavors. Enjoy the warmth and richness of this Thai classic! Adjust the level of spice and sourness to suit your taste preferences.

**Chicken and Dumplings**

Ingredients:

*For the Chicken Stew:*

- 1 whole chicken (about 4 pounds), cut into parts
- 2 tablespoons vegetable oil
- 1 onion, diced
- 3 carrots, sliced
- 3 celery stalks, sliced
- 3 cloves garlic, minced
- 1/4 cup all-purpose flour
- 6 cups chicken broth
- 1 cup frozen peas
- Salt and pepper to taste
- 1 teaspoon dried thyme
- 1 bay leaf
- 1/2 cup heavy cream (optional)

*For the Dumplings:*

- 2 cups all-purpose flour
- 1 tablespoon baking powder
- 1 teaspoon salt
- 1 cup whole milk
- 1/4 cup unsalted butter, melted

Instructions:

*For the Chicken Stew:*

Brown the Chicken:
- In a large pot, heat vegetable oil over medium-high heat. Brown the chicken pieces on all sides. Remove and set aside.

Sauté Vegetables:
- In the same pot, add diced onion, sliced carrots, sliced celery, and minced garlic. Sauté until the vegetables are softened.

Make Roux:

- Sprinkle flour over the vegetables and stir to create a roux. Cook for a couple of minutes to remove the raw taste of the flour.

Add Broth and Simmer:
- Gradually whisk in the chicken broth to avoid lumps. Add dried thyme, bay leaf, salt, and pepper. Bring the mixture to a simmer.

Add Chicken Back:
- Return the browned chicken to the pot. Cover and simmer for about 30-40 minutes until the chicken is cooked through.

Shred Chicken:
- Remove the chicken from the pot, shred the meat, and discard the bones. Return the shredded chicken to the pot.

Add Peas and Cream:
- Add frozen peas and heavy cream (if using). Simmer for an additional 10-15 minutes. Adjust seasoning if needed.

*For the Dumplings:*

Prepare Dumpling Dough:
- In a bowl, whisk together flour, baking powder, and salt. Add melted butter and milk, stirring just until combined.

Drop Dumplings:
- Drop spoonfuls of the dumpling batter onto the simmering stew. Cover and cook for about 15-20 minutes until the dumplings are cooked through.

Serve:
- Ladle the Chicken and Dumplings into bowls and serve hot.

This Chicken and Dumplings recipe creates a comforting and hearty dish that's perfect for cozy meals. Enjoy the combination of savory chicken, vegetables, and fluffy dumplings in a rich and flavorful broth!

**Roasted Garlic and Potato Soup**

Ingredients:

*For Roasted Garlic:*

- 1 head of garlic
- Olive oil
- Salt and pepper

*For Potato Soup:*

- 4 large russet potatoes, peeled and diced
- 1 onion, chopped
- 3 cloves garlic, minced
- 2 tablespoons butter
- 4 cups vegetable or chicken broth
- 1 cup whole milk or heavy cream
- Salt and pepper to taste
- Chives or green onions, chopped (for garnish)
- Grated cheddar cheese (optional, for garnish)

Instructions:

*For Roasted Garlic:*

Preheat Oven:
- Preheat your oven to 400°F (200°C).

Prepare Garlic Head:
- Cut off the top of the garlic head to expose the cloves. Place it on a piece of foil.

Drizzle with Olive Oil:
- Drizzle the exposed garlic cloves with olive oil and sprinkle with salt and pepper. Wrap the garlic in foil.

Roast Garlic:
- Roast in the preheated oven for about 30-40 minutes, or until the garlic cloves are soft and golden brown. Allow it to cool.

Squeeze Garlic:
- Once cooled, squeeze the roasted garlic cloves out of their skins and set aside.

*For Potato Soup:*

- Sauté Aromatics:
    - In a large pot, melt butter over medium heat. Add chopped onion and minced garlic. Sauté until the onion is translucent.
- Add Potatoes:
    - Add diced potatoes to the pot and cook for a few minutes, stirring occasionally.
- Pour in Broth:
    - Pour in the vegetable or chicken broth, ensuring that the potatoes are mostly covered. Bring the mixture to a simmer.
- Simmer Potatoes:
    - Let the potatoes simmer for about 15-20 minutes or until they are tender.
- Blend Soup:
    - Use an immersion blender to puree the soup until smooth. Alternatively, transfer the soup in batches to a blender and blend until smooth. Be cautious when blending hot liquids.
- Add Roasted Garlic:
    - Stir in the roasted garlic puree, incorporating it into the soup.
- Add Milk or Cream:
    - Pour in the whole milk or heavy cream. Stir well to combine.
- Season:
    - Season the soup with salt and pepper to taste.
- Heat Through:
    - Let the soup heat through, but do not boil once the dairy is added.
- Serve:
    - Ladle the Roasted Garlic and Potato Soup into bowls.
    - Garnish with chopped chives or green onions and grated cheddar cheese if desired.

This Roasted Garlic and Potato Soup is a comforting and flavorful option, perfect for a cozy meal. Enjoy the creamy texture and the depth of flavor from the roasted garlic!

**Wild Mushroom Bisque**

Ingredients:

- 1 pound mixed wild mushrooms (such as shiitake, oyster, and cremini), cleaned and chopped
- 1 onion, finely chopped
- 2 cloves garlic, minced
- 4 tablespoons unsalted butter
- 1/4 cup all-purpose flour
- 4 cups vegetable or chicken broth
- 1 cup dry white wine
- 1 cup heavy cream
- 1 teaspoon dried thyme
- Salt and pepper to taste
- Fresh chives, chopped (for garnish)
- Truffle oil (optional, for drizzling)

Instructions:

Sauté Mushrooms:
- In a large pot, melt 2 tablespoons of butter over medium heat. Add the chopped onions and sauté until softened. Add the minced garlic and sauté for an additional minute.
- Add the chopped wild mushrooms and cook until they release their moisture and become golden brown.

Make Roux:
- Push the mushrooms to one side of the pot and add the remaining 2 tablespoons of butter to the empty side. Once melted, sprinkle the flour over the butter and whisk to create a roux. Cook for 2-3 minutes to eliminate the raw flour taste.

Deglaze with Wine:
- Pour in the dry white wine to deglaze the pot, scraping up any browned bits from the bottom.

Add Broth and Thyme:
- Gradually whisk in the vegetable or chicken broth to the pot. Add dried thyme, salt, and pepper. Stir well to combine.

Simmer:

- Let the soup simmer for about 15-20 minutes, allowing the flavors to meld and the mushrooms to become tender.

Blend Soup:
- Use an immersion blender to puree the soup until smooth. Alternatively, transfer the soup in batches to a blender and blend until smooth. Be cautious when blending hot liquids.

Add Cream:
- Stir in the heavy cream and let the bisque simmer for an additional 5-10 minutes. Adjust the seasoning if necessary.

Serve:
- Ladle the Wild Mushroom Bisque into bowls.
- Garnish with chopped fresh chives and drizzle with truffle oil if desired.

This Wild Mushroom Bisque is a luxurious and elegant soup, perfect for special occasions or when you want to indulge in the rich flavors of wild mushrooms. Enjoy the creamy texture and depth of taste in each spoonful!

**Seafood Chowder**

Ingredients:

- 1/4 cup unsalted butter
- 1 onion, finely chopped
- 2 celery stalks, diced
- 2 carrots, peeled and diced
- 3 cloves garlic, minced
- 1/3 cup all-purpose flour
- 4 cups fish or seafood broth
- 1 cup clam juice
- 1 bay leaf
- 1 teaspoon dried thyme
- 1 teaspoon Old Bay seasoning
- 1 pound potatoes, peeled and diced
- 1 cup corn kernels (fresh or frozen)
- 1 cup diced cooked bacon or pancetta
- 1 pound mixed seafood (shrimp, scallops, crab, and/or white fish), peeled and deveined if necessary
- 2 cups heavy cream
- Salt and pepper to taste
- Fresh parsley, chopped (for garnish)

Instructions:

Sauté Vegetables:
- In a large pot, melt butter over medium heat. Add chopped onion, diced celery, diced carrots, and minced garlic. Sauté until the vegetables are softened.

Add Flour:
- Sprinkle flour over the vegetables and stir well to create a roux. Cook for 2-3 minutes to remove the raw taste of the flour.

Pour in Broth:
- Gradually whisk in fish or seafood broth and clam juice. Add the bay leaf, dried thyme, and Old Bay seasoning. Stir well to combine.

Add Potatoes and Corn:
- Add diced potatoes and corn kernels to the pot. Bring the mixture to a simmer and cook until the potatoes are tender.

Stir in Bacon:
- Stir in the diced cooked bacon or pancetta.

Add Seafood:
- Add the mixed seafood to the pot and cook until the seafood is just cooked through. Be careful not to overcook.

Pour in Cream:
- Pour in the heavy cream and stir well. Let the chowder simmer for an additional 5-10 minutes.

Season:
- Season the chowder with salt and pepper to taste. Adjust the seasoning as needed.

Serve:
- Ladle the Seafood Chowder into bowls.
- Garnish with chopped fresh parsley.

This Seafood Chowder is a delightful and indulgent soup that's perfect for seafood lovers. Enjoy the rich and creamy flavors of the chowder!

**Lemon Lentil Soup**

Ingredients:

- 1 cup dried red or green lentils, rinsed and drained
- 1 tablespoon olive oil
- 1 onion, finely chopped
- 3 carrots, peeled and diced
- 3 celery stalks, diced
- 3 cloves garlic, minced
- 1 teaspoon ground cumin
- 1 teaspoon ground coriander
- 1/2 teaspoon turmeric
- 6 cups vegetable or chicken broth
- 2 bay leaves
- Zest and juice of 2 lemons
- Salt and pepper to taste
- Fresh parsley, chopped (for garnish)
- Lemon slices (for serving)

Instructions:

Sauté Aromatics:
- In a large pot, heat olive oil over medium heat. Add chopped onion, diced carrots, diced celery, and minced garlic. Sauté until the vegetables are softened.

Add Spices:
- Stir in ground cumin, ground coriander, and turmeric. Cook for an additional 1-2 minutes to toast the spices.

Add Lentils and Broth:
- Add rinsed lentils to the pot. Pour in the vegetable or chicken broth. Stir well.

Add Bay Leaves:
- Add bay leaves to the pot. Bring the mixture to a boil, then reduce the heat and let it simmer for about 20-25 minutes or until the lentils are tender.

Zest and Juice Lemons:
- While the soup is simmering, zest and juice the lemons.

Add Lemon Zest and Juice:

- Stir in the lemon zest and juice. Adjust the amount to your taste preference.

Season:
- Season the soup with salt and pepper to taste. Remove the bay leaves.

Serve:
- Ladle the Lemon Lentil Soup into bowls.
- Garnish with chopped fresh parsley and serve with lemon slices on the side.

This Lemon Lentil Soup is a light and flavorful option, perfect for a refreshing meal. The combination of lentils and citrusy lemon creates a satisfying and comforting bowl of soup. Enjoy!

**Mexican Street Corn Soup**

Ingredients:

- 4 cups fresh or frozen corn kernels
- 2 tablespoons olive oil
- 1 onion, finely chopped
- 2 cloves garlic, minced
- 1 jalapeño, seeds removed and finely chopped
- 1 teaspoon ground cumin
- 1 teaspoon chili powder
- 4 cups vegetable or chicken broth
- 1 can (14 ounces) diced tomatoes, undrained
- 1 cup whole milk or heavy cream
- Juice of 1 lime
- Salt and pepper to taste
- Cotija cheese, crumbled (for garnish)
- Fresh cilantro, chopped (for garnish)
- Lime wedges (for serving)

Instructions:

Char Corn:
- In a large skillet over medium-high heat, char the corn kernels in batches with a little olive oil until they have a nice golden color. Set aside.

Sauté Aromatics:
- In a large pot, heat olive oil over medium heat. Add chopped onion, minced garlic, and chopped jalapeño. Sauté until the vegetables are softened.

Add Spices:
- Stir in ground cumin and chili powder. Cook for an additional 1-2 minutes to toast the spices.

Pour in Broth and Tomatoes:
- Add vegetable or chicken broth to the pot. Pour in diced tomatoes with their juices. Bring the mixture to a simmer.

Blend:
- Use an immersion blender to puree the soup until smooth. Alternatively, transfer the soup in batches to a blender and blend until smooth. Be cautious when blending hot liquids.

Add Charred Corn:

- Stir in the charred corn kernels.

**Pour in Milk or Cream:**
- Pour in whole milk or heavy cream. Stir well.

**Add Lime Juice:**
- Squeeze in the juice of one lime and stir to incorporate.

**Season:**
- Season the soup with salt and pepper to taste.

**Simmer:**
- Let the soup simmer for an additional 10-15 minutes to allow the flavors to meld.

**Serve:**
- Ladle the Mexican Street Corn Soup into bowls.
- Garnish with crumbled Cotija cheese and chopped fresh cilantro.
- Serve with lime wedges on the side.

This Mexican Street Corn Soup is a flavorful and creamy delight, perfect for capturing the essence of elote in a comforting bowl. Enjoy the vibrant flavors of Mexican street corn in this delicious soup!

**Tuscan White Bean Soup**

Ingredients:

- 2 tablespoons olive oil
- 1 onion, chopped
- 2 carrots, peeled and diced
- 2 celery stalks, diced
- 3 cloves garlic, minced
- 2 teaspoons dried rosemary
- 1 teaspoon dried thyme
- 2 cans (15 ounces each) cannellini beans, drained and rinsed
- 4 cups vegetable or chicken broth
- 1 can (14 ounces) diced tomatoes, undrained
- 1 bunch kale, stems removed and leaves chopped
- Salt and pepper to taste
- Grated Parmesan cheese (for serving)
- Crusty bread (for serving)

Instructions:

Sauté Vegetables:
- In a large pot, heat olive oil over medium heat. Add chopped onion, diced carrots, diced celery, and minced garlic. Sauté until the vegetables are softened.

Add Herbs and Beans:
- Stir in dried rosemary and dried thyme. Add cannellini beans and mix well.

Pour in Broth:
- Pour in vegetable or chicken broth and bring the mixture to a simmer.

Incorporate Tomatoes:
- Add diced tomatoes (with their juices) to the pot. Stir to combine.

Simmer:
- Let the soup simmer for about 15-20 minutes to allow the flavors to meld.

Add Kale:
- Add chopped kale to the pot and cook until wilted.

Season:
- Season the soup with salt and pepper to taste.

Serve:

- Ladle the Tuscan White Bean Soup into bowls.
- Garnish with grated Parmesan cheese.
- Serve with crusty bread on the side.

This Tuscan White Bean Soup is a comforting and nutritious option, perfect for a satisfying meal. Enjoy the combination of creamy white beans, aromatic herbs, and hearty vegetables in this delicious soup!

**Roasted Pumpkin and Sage Soup**

Ingredients:

- 1 small pumpkin (about 3-4 pounds), peeled, seeded, and cut into chunks
- 2 tablespoons olive oil
- Salt and pepper to taste
- 1 onion, chopped
- 2 cloves garlic, minced
- 1 teaspoon dried sage (or 2 teaspoons fresh sage, chopped)
- 4 cups vegetable or chicken broth
- 1 potato, peeled and diced
- 1 carrot, peeled and diced
- 1 apple, peeled, cored, and diced
- 1/2 teaspoon ground cinnamon
- 1/4 teaspoon ground nutmeg
- 1 cup milk or cream (optional, for creaminess)
- Fresh sage leaves (for garnish)

Instructions:

Roast Pumpkin:
- Preheat the oven to 400°F (200°C).
- Toss the pumpkin chunks with olive oil, salt, and pepper. Spread them on a baking sheet.
- Roast in the preheated oven for about 30-40 minutes or until the pumpkin is tender and slightly caramelized.

Sauté Aromatics:
- In a large pot, heat a bit of olive oil over medium heat. Add chopped onion and cook until softened.
- Add minced garlic and dried sage (or fresh sage) and cook for an additional 1-2 minutes until fragrant.

Add Broth and Vegetables:
- Pour in vegetable or chicken broth. Add diced potato, diced carrot, and diced apple to the pot.
- Bring the mixture to a simmer and cook until the vegetables are tender.

Blend Soup:

- Add the roasted pumpkin chunks to the pot. Use an immersion blender to puree the soup until smooth. Alternatively, transfer the soup in batches to a blender and blend until smooth. Be cautious when blending hot liquids.

Season:
- Stir in ground cinnamon and ground nutmeg. Season the soup with salt and pepper to taste.

Add Milk or Cream (Optional):
- For added creaminess, stir in milk or cream. Adjust the consistency to your liking.

Simmer:
- Let the soup simmer for an additional 5-10 minutes to allow the flavors to meld.

Serve:
- Ladle the Roasted Pumpkin and Sage Soup into bowls.
- Garnish with fresh sage leaves.

This Roasted Pumpkin and Sage Soup is a warm and comforting option, perfect for embracing the flavors of the season. Enjoy the rich and earthy taste of roasted pumpkin combined with the aromatic notes of sage!

**Chicken Gumbo**

Ingredients:

- 1/2 cup vegetable oil
- 1/2 cup all-purpose flour
- 1 large onion, chopped
- 1 bell pepper, chopped
- 2 celery stalks, chopped
- 3 cloves garlic, minced
- 1 pound boneless, skinless chicken thighs, cut into bite-sized pieces
- 1 pound andouille sausage, sliced
- 1 can (14 ounces) diced tomatoes, undrained
- 1 can (10 ounces) diced tomatoes with green chilies (Rotel), undrained
- 4 cups chicken broth
- 1 teaspoon dried thyme
- 1 teaspoon dried oregano
- 1 teaspoon smoked paprika
- 1/2 teaspoon cayenne pepper (adjust to taste)
- Salt and pepper to taste
- 1 bay leaf
- 1 cup okra, sliced (fresh or frozen)
- 1 cup frozen sliced okra (optional)
- 1 cup frozen sliced okra (optional)
- Cooked rice for serving
- Chopped green onions for garnish

Instructions:

Make Roux:
- In a large, heavy-bottomed pot, combine vegetable oil and flour over medium heat to make a roux. Stir continuously for about 20-30 minutes until the roux turns a dark, chocolate brown color.

Sauté Vegetables:
- Add chopped onion, bell pepper, celery, and minced garlic to the roux. Cook for an additional 5-7 minutes until the vegetables are softened.

Add Chicken and Sausage:
- Add the cut chicken and sliced andouille sausage to the pot. Cook until the chicken is browned on all sides.

Incorporate Tomatoes:
- Stir in diced tomatoes, diced tomatoes with green chilies, and their juices. Mix well.

Pour in Broth:
- Pour in chicken broth, ensuring that the meats and vegetables are covered. Stir to combine.

Add Spices:
- Add dried thyme, dried oregano, smoked paprika, cayenne pepper, salt, and pepper. Drop in the bay leaf. Mix well.

Simmer:
- Bring the mixture to a simmer, then reduce the heat to low. Let it simmer for about 1-2 hours, allowing the flavors to meld.

Add Okra:
- Add sliced okra to the pot. Continue simmering for an additional 30 minutes.

Adjust Seasoning:
- Taste and adjust the seasoning, adding more salt, pepper, or cayenne pepper as needed.

Serve:
- Remove the bay leaf before serving.
- Serve the Chicken Gumbo over cooked rice.
- Garnish with chopped green onions.

This Chicken Gumbo is a comforting and flavorful dish that brings the taste of Louisiana to your table. Enjoy the rich and spicy flavors of this classic Southern stew!

**Tomato and Basil Bisque**

Ingredients:

- 2 tablespoons olive oil
- 1 onion, chopped
- 3 cloves garlic, minced
- 2 cans (28 ounces each) whole tomatoes, undrained
- 1 can (14 ounces) diced tomatoes, undrained
- 1/4 cup tomato paste
- 1 cup vegetable broth
- 1 cup heavy cream
- 1/2 cup fresh basil leaves, chopped
- Salt and pepper to taste
- Pinch of sugar (optional, to balance acidity)
- Grated Parmesan cheese (for garnish, optional)
- Croutons (for garnish, optional)

Instructions:

Sauté Aromatics:
- In a large pot, heat olive oil over medium heat. Add chopped onion and cook until softened.
- Add minced garlic and sauté for an additional 1-2 minutes until fragrant.

Add Tomatoes:
- Pour in whole tomatoes and diced tomatoes with their juices. Break up the whole tomatoes with a spoon or spatula.

Incorporate Tomato Paste:
- Stir in tomato paste to enhance the tomato flavor. Mix well.

Pour in Broth:
- Add vegetable broth to the pot. Bring the mixture to a simmer.

Blend Soup:
- Use an immersion blender to puree the soup until smooth. Alternatively, transfer the soup in batches to a blender and blend until smooth. Be cautious when blending hot liquids.

Add Heavy Cream:
- Pour in heavy cream, stirring continuously to combine.

Add Basil:

- Stir in chopped fresh basil. Reserve a small amount for garnish if desired.

Season:
- Season the bisque with salt and pepper to taste. Add a pinch of sugar if needed to balance acidity.

Simmer:
- Let the Tomato and Basil Bisque simmer for an additional 10-15 minutes to allow the flavors to meld.

Serve:
- Ladle the bisque into bowls.
- Garnish with additional fresh basil, grated Parmesan cheese, and croutons if desired.

This Tomato and Basil Bisque is a creamy and indulgent soup, perfect for a comforting meal. Enjoy the rich flavors of ripe tomatoes and aromatic basil in every spoonful!

**Black Bean and Chorizo Soup**

Ingredients:

- 1 tablespoon olive oil
- 1 onion, chopped
- 2 cloves garlic, minced
- 1 pound chorizo sausage, casing removed and crumbled
- 2 cans (15 ounces each) black beans, drained and rinsed
- 1 can (14 ounces) diced tomatoes, undrained
- 4 cups chicken or vegetable broth
- 1 teaspoon ground cumin
- 1 teaspoon chili powder
- 1/2 teaspoon smoked paprika
- Salt and pepper to taste
- Juice of 1 lime
- Fresh cilantro, chopped (for garnish)
- Sour cream or Greek yogurt (optional, for serving)
- Sliced jalapeños (optional, for serving)

Instructions:

Sauté Aromatics:
- In a large pot, heat olive oil over medium heat. Add chopped onion and cook until softened.
- Add minced garlic and sauté for an additional 1-2 minutes until fragrant.

Cook Chorizo:
- Add crumbled chorizo to the pot. Cook until the chorizo is browned and cooked through.

Add Beans and Tomatoes:
- Stir in black beans and diced tomatoes (with their juices).

Pour in Broth:
- Add chicken or vegetable broth to the pot. Bring the mixture to a simmer.

Season:
- Add ground cumin, chili powder, smoked paprika, salt, and pepper. Stir well to combine.

Simmer:
- Let the soup simmer for about 15-20 minutes to allow the flavors to meld.

Finish with Lime Juice:
- Squeeze in the juice of one lime. Stir well.

Adjust Seasoning:
- Taste the soup and adjust the seasoning, adding more salt or spices if needed.

Serve:
- Ladle the Black Bean and Chorizo Soup into bowls.
- Garnish with chopped fresh cilantro.
- Serve with a dollop of sour cream or Greek yogurt and sliced jalapeños if desired.

This Black Bean and Chorizo Soup is a robust and flavorful option, perfect for a satisfying and spicy meal. Enjoy the combination of smoky chorizo, hearty black beans, and aromatic spices!

**Lemon Artichoke Soup**

Ingredients:

- 2 tablespoons olive oil
- 1 onion, chopped
- 2 cloves garlic, minced
- 1 can (14 ounces) artichoke hearts, drained and chopped
- 1 potato, peeled and diced
- 4 cups vegetable broth
- 1/2 cup fresh lemon juice (about 2-3 lemons)
- Zest of 1 lemon
- 1 teaspoon dried thyme
- 1/2 teaspoon dried oregano
- Salt and pepper to taste
- 1 cup spinach or kale, chopped
- 1/2 cup heavy cream or coconut milk (optional, for creaminess)
- Fresh parsley, chopped (for garnish)

Instructions:

Sauté Aromatics:
- In a large pot, heat olive oil over medium heat. Add chopped onion and cook until softened.
- Add minced garlic and sauté for an additional 1-2 minutes until fragrant.

Add Artichokes and Potato:
- Stir in chopped artichoke hearts and diced potato.

Pour in Broth:
- Add vegetable broth to the pot. Bring the mixture to a simmer.

Incorporate Lemon:
- Add fresh lemon juice, lemon zest, dried thyme, dried oregano, salt, and pepper. Stir well to combine.

Simmer:
- Let the soup simmer for about 15-20 minutes or until the potato is tender.

Add Greens:
- Stir in chopped spinach or kale and cook until wilted.

Blend Soup:

- Use an immersion blender to puree the soup until smooth. Alternatively, transfer the soup in batches to a blender and blend until smooth. Be cautious when blending hot liquids.

Add Cream (Optional):
- Stir in heavy cream or coconut milk if you desire added creaminess.

Adjust Seasoning:
- Taste the soup and adjust the seasoning, adding more salt, pepper, or lemon juice if needed.

Serve:
- Ladle the Lemon Artichoke Soup into bowls.
- Garnish with chopped fresh parsley.

This Lemon Artichoke Soup is a light and vibrant option, perfect for a refreshing and citrusy meal. Enjoy the combination of lemony brightness and the unique flavor of artichokes in this delicious soup!

**Hungarian Goulash Soup**

Ingredients:

- 2 tablespoons vegetable oil
- 1 large onion, finely chopped
- 2 cloves garlic, minced
- 1 1/2 pounds beef stew meat, cut into bite-sized pieces
- 2 tablespoons sweet paprika
- 1 teaspoon caraway seeds
- 2 tablespoons tomato paste
- 4 cups beef broth
- 2 medium potatoes, peeled and diced
- 2 carrots, peeled and sliced
- 1 red bell pepper, chopped
- 1 green bell pepper, chopped
- 1 can (14 ounces) diced tomatoes, undrained
- Salt and pepper to taste
- 2 tablespoons all-purpose flour (optional, for thickening)
- Sour cream (for serving)
- Chopped fresh parsley (for garnish)

Instructions:

Sauté Aromatics:
- In a large pot, heat vegetable oil over medium heat. Add chopped onion and cook until softened.
- Add minced garlic and cook for an additional 1-2 minutes until fragrant.

Cook Beef:
- Add beef stew meat to the pot. Cook until browned on all sides.

Add Paprika and Caraway Seeds:
- Sprinkle sweet paprika and caraway seeds over the beef. Stir well to coat the meat in the spices.

Incorporate Tomato Paste:
- Stir in tomato paste and cook for 1-2 minutes to enhance the flavor.

Pour in Broth:
- Add beef broth to the pot. Bring the mixture to a simmer.

Add Vegetables:

- Add diced potatoes, sliced carrots, chopped red bell pepper, and chopped green bell pepper to the pot.

Incorporate Tomatoes:
- Stir in diced tomatoes with their juices. Season with salt and pepper to taste.

Simmer:
- Let the soup simmer for about 1 to 1.5 hours, or until the beef is tender and the vegetables are cooked.

Optional Thickening:
- If you prefer a thicker soup, mix 2 tablespoons of flour with a bit of water to create a slurry. Stir the slurry into the soup and simmer until thickened.

Serve:
- Ladle the Hungarian Goulash Soup into bowls.
- Garnish with a dollop of sour cream and chopped fresh parsley.

This Hungarian Goulash Soup is a comforting and flavorful option, perfect for a satisfying meal. Enjoy the rich taste of paprika and the tender beef in every spoonful!

**Spaghetti Squash and Meatball Soup**

Ingredients:

*For Meatballs:*

- 1 pound ground beef (or a mixture of beef and pork)
- 1/2 cup breadcrumbs
- 1/4 cup grated Parmesan cheese
- 1/4 cup chopped fresh parsley
- 1 egg
- 2 cloves garlic, minced
- Salt and pepper to taste
- Olive oil for cooking

*For Soup:*

- 1 medium-sized spaghetti squash
- 1 tablespoon olive oil
- 1 onion, chopped
- 2 carrots, peeled and sliced
- 2 celery stalks, sliced
- 3 cloves garlic, minced
- 6 cups beef or vegetable broth
- 1 can (14 ounces) diced tomatoes, undrained
- 1 teaspoon dried oregano
- 1 teaspoon dried basil
- Salt and pepper to taste
- Fresh basil or parsley for garnish
- Grated Parmesan cheese for serving

Instructions:

*For Meatballs:*

Prepare Meatball Mixture:
- In a bowl, combine ground beef, breadcrumbs, grated Parmesan, chopped parsley, egg, minced garlic, salt, and pepper. Mix until well combined.

Form Meatballs:
- Shape the mixture into small meatballs, about 1 inch in diameter.

Cook Meatballs:
- In a skillet, heat olive oil over medium heat. Cook the meatballs until browned on all sides and cooked through. Set aside.

*For Soup:*

Prepare Spaghetti Squash:
- Preheat the oven to 400°F (200°C). Cut the spaghetti squash in half lengthwise and scoop out the seeds. Place the squash, cut side down, on a baking sheet. Roast in the oven for about 40-45 minutes or until the squash is fork-tender. Scrape the flesh with a fork to create "spaghetti."

Sauté Aromatics:
- In a large pot, heat olive oil over medium heat. Add chopped onion, sliced carrots, sliced celery, and minced garlic. Sauté until the vegetables are softened.

Add Broth and Tomatoes:
- Pour in beef or vegetable broth. Add diced tomatoes with their juices. Bring the mixture to a simmer.

Season and Add Herbs:
- Season the soup with dried oregano, dried basil, salt, and pepper. Stir well to combine.

Add Meatballs and Spaghetti Squash:
- Add the cooked meatballs and the roasted spaghetti squash to the pot. Let the soup simmer for about 10-15 minutes to allow the flavors to meld.

Adjust Seasoning:
- Taste the soup and adjust the seasoning if needed.

Serve:
- Ladle the Spaghetti Squash and Meatball Soup into bowls.
- Garnish with fresh basil or parsley and serve with grated Parmesan cheese on the side.

This Spaghetti Squash and Meatball Soup is a satisfying and wholesome meal, combining the comfort of meatballs with the unique texture of spaghetti squash. Enjoy this nutritious twist on a classic soup!

www.ingramcontent.com/pod-product-compliance
Lightning Source LLC
LaVergne TN
LVHW061942070526
838199LV00060B/3923